EGYPTIAN MYTHOLOGY

HORUS

BY ALYSSA KREKELBERG

CONTENT CONSULTANT
KASIA SZPAKOWSKA, PhD
PROFESSOR EMERITUS OF EGYPTOLOGY

Kids Core
An Imprint of Abdo Publishing
abdobooks.com

abdobooks.com

Published by Abdo Publishing, a division of ABDO, PO Box 398166, Minneapolis, Minnesota 55439. Copyright © 2023 by Abdo Consulting Group, Inc. International copyrights reserved in all countries. No part of this book may be reproduced in any form without written permission from the publisher. Kids Core™ is a trademark and logo of Abdo Publishing.

Printed in the United States of America, North Mankato, Minnesota.
052022
092022

Cover Photos: Olga Chernyak/Shutterstock Images, Horus; Shutterstock Images, background
Interior Photos: Guido Vermeulen-Perdaen/Shutterstock Images, 4–5, 29 (top); Shutterstock Images, 6, 28 (bottom); Guenter Albers/Shutterstock Images, 9; The Print Collector/Alamy, 10; Falkenstein Foto/Alamy, 12–13; Paul Vinten/Shutterstock Images, 15, 28 (top); Vladimir Zadvinskii/Shutterstock Images, 16; Peter Hermes Furian/Shutterstock Images, 18; Michele Falzone/Jon Arnold Images Ltd/Alamy, 20–21; Nick Brundle Photography/Shutterstock Images, 22; Artokoloro/Alamy, 25; Anton Ivanov/Shutterstock Images, 26, 29 (bottom)

Editor: Layna Darling
Series Designer: Ryan Gale

Library of Congress Control Number: 2021952339

Publisher's Cataloging-in-Publication Data

Names: Krekelberg, Alyssa, author.
Title: Horus / by Alyssa Krekelberg
Description: Minneapolis, Minnesota : Abdo Publishing, 2023 | Series: Egyptian mythology | Includes online resources and index.
Identifiers: ISBN 9781532198670 (lib. bdg.) | ISBN 9781644947753 (pbk.) | ISBN 9781098272326 (ebook)
Subjects: LCSH: Horus (Egyptian deity)--Juvenile literature. | Egypt--Religion--Juvenile literature. | Gods, Egyptian--Juvenile literature. | Mythology, Egyptian--Juvenile literature.
Classification: DDC 932.01--dc23

CONTENTS

CHAPTER 1
Taking the Throne 4

CHAPTER 2
The King of Egypt 12

CHAPTER 3
Horus in Ancient Egypt 20

Legendary Facts 28
Glossary 30
Online Resources 31
Learn More 31
Index 32
About the Author 32

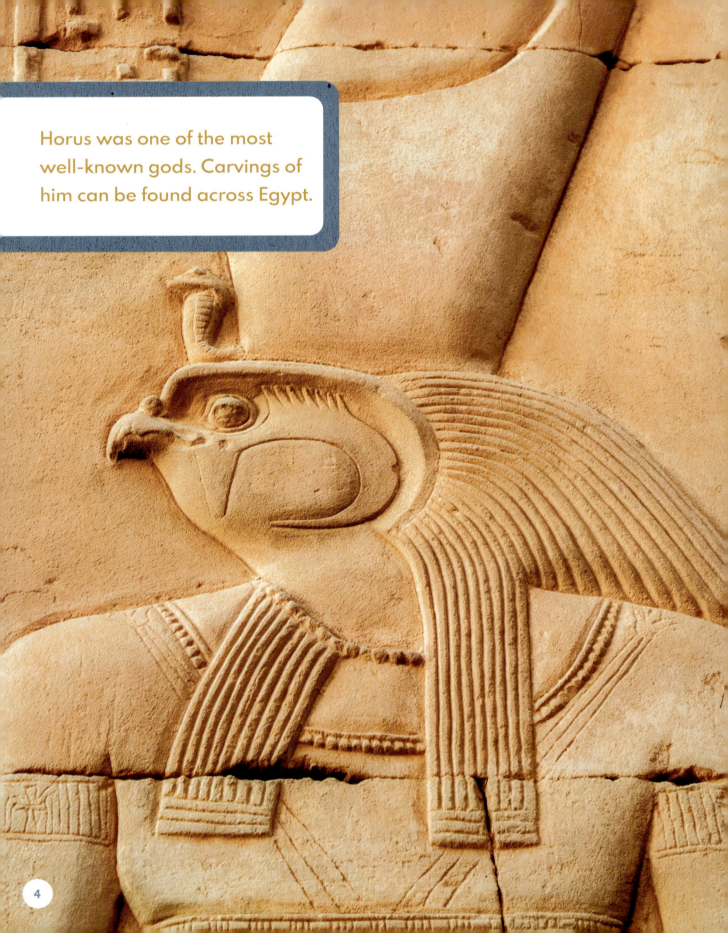

Horus was one of the most well-known gods. Carvings of him can be found across Egypt.

TAKING THE THRONE

Horus stood before the Egyptian gods. He told them that he was the true ruler of Egypt. His father, the god Osiris, was king before Horus was born. Then the god Seth killed Osiris and tried to take the throne for himself. Seth was Horus's uncle.

Horus, *right*, battled his uncle Seth, *left*, for control of the Egyptian throne.

Many of the gods thought Horus should be king. But Seth argued that there should be a contest to decide who got to rule Egypt. The gods agreed.

For the next 80 years, Horus and Seth battled each other in different ways. Once, they decided to race stone ships. But Horus secretly made his ship out of wood. That way, it would float on water while his uncle's boat sank. Horus disguised his ship so no one would know. Another time, Horus and Seth fought with weapons. Seth damaged Horus's left eye. The god Thoth fixed it, and Horus didn't give up.

Eye of Horus

Horus had magical eyes. His right eye was the sun. His left was the moon. The story of Seth hurting Horus's left eye explained a natural event. The ancient Egyptians believed the damaged eye explained the phases of the moon. They also created images of Horus's left eye. This was called the Eye of Horus. It represented health and protection.

He won each contest against his uncle. Eventually, Horus became the king of Egypt.

Egyptian Myths

Ancient Egypt was a **civilization** in northeastern Africa. It existed around 5,000 years ago. A pharaoh, or king, ruled over ancient Egypt. During that time, people thought the pharaohs were gods.

The ancient Egyptians wanted to understand the world around them. They asked questions about how the world formed. They wanted to know why the sun rose and set each day. They wondered whether there was life after death. Stories of powerful gods and goddesses helped answer these questions.

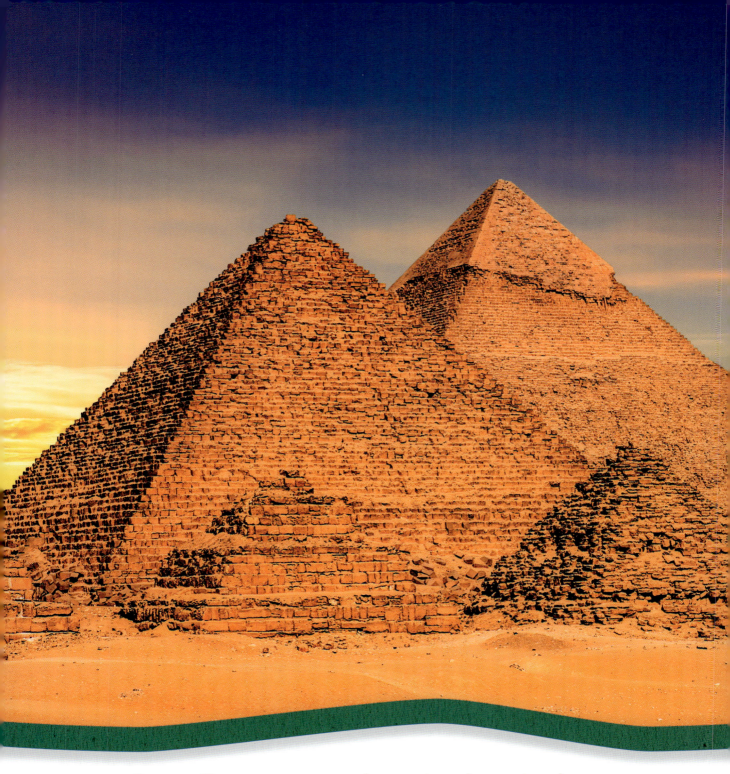

Ancient Egypt was a complex society that existed around 5,000 years ago. Some of the structures built by ancient Egyptians still stand today.

Ancient Egyptians told myths about gods and goddesses to understand the events around them.

Ancient Egyptians thought the gods created the world. They believed the gods could impact people's lives. They told stories about the gods that are known today as Egyptian myths. Horus was one of the most well-known gods. He had a strong connection to Egyptian pharaohs.

PRIMARY SOURCE

The authors of a 2019 study described the importance of the battle of Horus and Seth:

> The ancient Egyptians used this legendary fight as a [**symbol**] of the battle between good and evil, order and **chaos**. Afterward, Horus was [worshipped] by the ancient Egyptians in the form of the Eye of Horus.

Source: Karim ReFaey et al. "The Eye of Horus: The Connection Between Art, Medicine, and Mythology in Ancient Egypt." *Cureus*, May 2019, vol. 11, no. 5, ncbi.nlm.nih.gov. Accessed 1 Oct. 2021.

Comparing Texts

Think about the quote. Does it support the information in this chapter or give a different perspective? Explain how in a few sentences.

Horus, *left*, was the son of Osiris, *center*, and Isis, *right*.

CHAPTER 2

THE KING OF EGYPT

Horus was the son of the powerful **deities** Isis and Osiris. After Osiris was killed, Isis fled to the **marshes** of the Nile River. She was pregnant with Horus, and Seth wanted to kill him. Seth didn't want Horus to grow up and take the throne of Egypt.

Horus faced dangerous creatures in the marshes. Scorpions, crocodiles, and snakes bit him. Sometimes he was poisoned by these animals. But his mother was a powerful healer. She used her magic to cure him.

Close to Death

One day, Isis went searching for food. She left Horus alone in the marshes. Suddenly, he

Changing Myths

Stories about mythological characters can change over time. For instance, some myths say the goddess Hathor was Horus's mother. Other stories say she was his wife. Hathor was the goddess of love, **fertility**, women, and the sky. Her name means "the house of Horus."

Isis hid Horus in the marshes of the Nile River.

heard a rustling in the weeds. A snake slithered toward him. It was Seth. He had finally found Horus and had used his own magical powers to transform into a snake. Seth attacked and poisoned Horus.

Many goddesses helped Horus become strong enough to beat Seth.

When Isis came back, she was horrified to find her son half dead. She realized she couldn't cure Horus on her own. But she would do anything to save him. She called on the other gods for help. They aided her, and Horus was saved.

Growing Up

Some stories say that when Horus was young, other goddesses tried to help him. For instance, Selket was a scorpion goddess of protection. She created seven scorpions to protect Isis and Horus. The scorpions followed the pair around. They tried to protect Isis and Horus from danger. Selket also helped teach Horus. She wanted him to be strong enough to one day beat Seth.

A Divided Egypt

Lower and Upper Egypt are geographic places. Lower Egypt is in the north, and Upper Egypt is in the south. This is because the regions are named for the flow of the Nile River. The river flows from south to north. Lower Egypt has healthy soil to grow crops. Upper Egypt is near the desert. In 3100 BCE, a man named Narmer united Lower and Upper Egypt. He became the king. People believed he was Horus reborn.

After Horus grew up, he confronted his uncle. The conflict between Horus and Seth lasted for a long time. Some myths say that at one point, the gods decided Egypt should be divided. They gave Lower Egypt to Horus. They gave Upper Egypt to Seth. But this division didn't work out well. Eventually Horus became the ruler of all Egypt. He was a wise king. He brought order back to Egypt after Seth's chaotic rule.

Explore Online

Visit the website below. Does it give any new information about Horus that wasn't in Chapter Two?

Horus
abdocorelibrary.com/horus

Horus, *left*, was often connected to Egyptian pharaohs. He is pictured here with Horemheb, who ruled ancient Egypt from 1319–1292 BCE.

HORUS IN ANCIENT EGYPT

People thought pharaohs were **manifestations** of Horus. A pharaoh got five names when he rose to power. One was a Horus name. The pharaoh Thutmose III's Horus name was Kanakht Khaemwaset. This name was written on the pharaoh's tomb.

Horus is often shown as a falcon.

The Falcon God

Horus was one of the most important gods in ancient Egypt. Horus was known as the falcon-headed god. Falcons are birds of prey. They are fast and strong. In artwork, Horus is often shown as having a man's body with a falcon's head. The Eye of Horus is the same shape as the markings around a falcon's eye. Horus is also seen as a falcon wearing a crown.

In his full falcon form, his speckled feathers represented the stars. His wings were the sky.

In ancient Egypt, the falcon was a symbol of the pharaoh. Some ancient writings talk about how Egypt's enemies felt scared when facing the pharaoh. They believed this was how other birds felt when seeing a falcon.

The Cobra and the Double Crown

Some artwork of Horus shows him with a cobra. This animal is a symbol of protection. It was thought to help keep him from harm. Also, Horus often wears a double crown. One piece represents Lower Egypt, and one piece represents Upper Egypt. Pharaohs often wore double crowns too.

In artwork, Horus's falcon form often flies above images of the pharaohs. This was a way of showing how the pharaohs were connected to the gods.

Some ancient Egyptians carved falcons on tombs. Some coffins were falcon shaped. People sometimes even mummified real falcons. Then they buried the falcons with the dead. They did this to show how important Horus was to them.

Temples and Worship

The ancient Egyptians built many temples to honor Horus. One was the Temple of Horus at Edfu. It was built between 237 and 57 BCE. The temple is very well-preserved. People can visit it today. Carvings are found inside. They show

Ancient Egyptians would mummify falcons to honor the gods. Sometimes, they would place them in a box decorated with Horus in his falcon form.

the conflict between Horus and Seth. Historians think the story was acted out by ancient Egyptians at the temple every year.

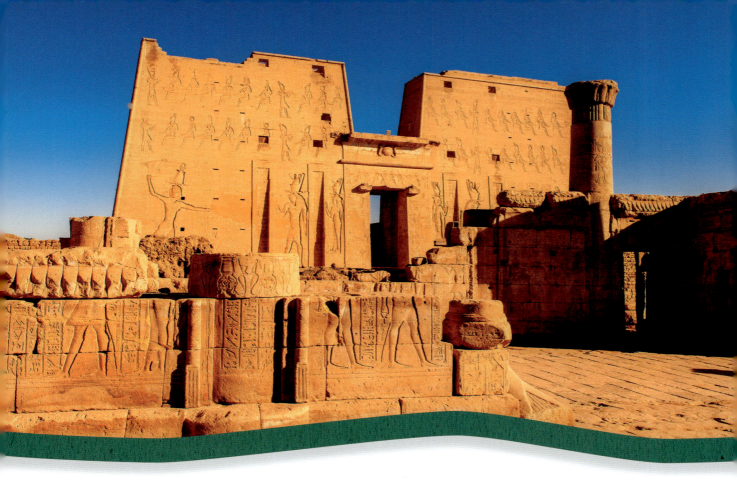

Egyptians honored Horus at a temple dedicated to him in Edfu. People can visit it today.

Ancient Egyptians worshipped Horus in their temples. At Edfu, they held ceremonies to honor the god. One was called the Coronation of the Sacred Falcon. It was held every year. During this celebration, a real falcon was chosen to represent Horus.

Horus Today

Images of Horus are commonly seen in Egypt today. The falcon-headed god's image appears on the sides of airplanes. It is also used in restaurants and hotels. Stories of Horus were first told thousands of years ago. But his myths and image continue to live on today.

Further Evidence

Look at the website below. Does it give any new evidence to support Chapter Three?

Ancient Egyptian Temples
abdocorelibrary.com/horus

LEGENDARY FACTS

When Horus was a child, he lived in the marshes of the Nile River. He was hiding from his cruel uncle, Seth.

As an adult, Horus battled Seth for control of Egypt and won.

In artwork, Horus is often seen as either a man with a falcon's head or as a falcon.

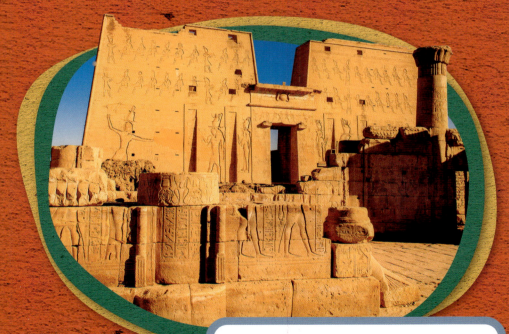

Ancient Egyptians built temples to honor Horus. They held celebrations there.

Glossary

chaos
disorder and confusion

civilization
a complex, organized society

deities
gods or goddesses

fertility
the ability to produce young or new life

manifestations
visible representations of beings or ideas

marshes
areas of muddy, wet land

symbol
an object that represents a certain quality or idea

Online Resources

To learn more about Horus, visit our free resource websites below.

Visit **abdocorelibrary.com** or scan this QR code for free Common Core resources for teachers and students, including vetted activities, multimedia, and booklinks, for deeper subject comprehension.

Visit **abdobooklinks.com** or scan this QR code for free additional online weblinks for further learning. These links are routinely monitored and updated to provide the most current information available.

Learn More

Hudak, Heather C. *Seth*. Abdo, 2023.

McDonald, Angela. *Ancient Egypt*. DK, 2017.

Index

Edfu, 24, 26
Eye of Horus, 7, 11, 22

falcons, 22–24, 26–27

Hathor, 14

Isis, 13–14, 17

Lower Egypt, 18–19, 23

marshes, 13–14

Nile River, 13, 18

Osiris, 5, 13

pharaohs, 8, 10, 21, 23–24

scorpions, 14, 17
Seth, 5–7, 11, 13, 15, 17, 19, 25

temples, 24–27
Thoth, 7
Thutmose III, 21

Upper Egypt, 18–19, 23

About the Author

Alyssa Krekelberg has been fascinated with Egyptian mythology since elementary school. She lives in Minnesota, where she writes and edits books for young readers.